theatre & time

Theatre &
Series Editors: Jen Harvie and Dan Rebellato

Published
Susan Bennett: *Theatre & Museums*
Bill Blake: *Theatre & the Digital*
Colette Conroy: *Theatre & the Body*
Emma Cox: *Theatre & Migration*
Jill Dolan: *Theatre & Sexuality*
Helen Freshwater: *Theatre & Audience*
Jen Harvie: *Theatre & the City*
Nadine Holdsworth: *Theatre & Nation*
Erin Hurley: *Theatre & Feeling*
Dominic Johnson: *Theatre & the Visual*
Joe Kelleher: *Theatre & Politics*
Ric Knowles: *Theatre & Interculturalism*
Caoimhe McAvinchey: *Theatre & Prison*
Bruce McConachie: *Theatre & Mind*
Lucy Nevitt: *Theatre & Violence*
Helen Nicholson: *Theatre & Education*
Lourdes Orozco: *Theatre & Animals*
Lionel Pilkington: *Theatre & Ireland*
Paul Rae: *Theatre & Human Rights*
Dan Rebellato: *Theatre & Globalization*
Trish Reid: *Theatre & Scotland*
Nicholas Ridout: *Theatre & Ethics*
Rebecca Schneider: *Theatre & History*
Fintan Walsh: *Theatre & Therapy*
David Wiles: *Theatre & Time*
Harvey Young: *Theatre & Race*

Forthcoming
Jim Davis: *Theatre & Entertainment*
Eric Weitz: *Theatre & Laughter*

Theatre&
Series Standing Order ISBN 978–0–230–20327–3

You can receive future titles in this series as they are published by placing a standing order. Please contact your bookseller or, in case of difficulty, write to us at the address below with your name and address, the title of the series and the ISBN quoted above.

Customer Services Department, Macmillan Distribution Ltd, Houndmills, Basingstoke, Hampshire, RG21 6XS, UK

---

theatre & time

David Wiles

palgrave
macmillan

First published 2014 by
PALGRAVE MACMILLAN

Palgrave Macmillan in the UK is an imprint of Macmillan Publishers Limited, registered in England, company number 785998, of Houndmills, Basingstoke, Hampshire RG21 6XS.

Palgrave Macmillan in the US is a division of St Martin's Press LLC, 175 Fifth Avenue, New York, NY 10010.

Palgrave Macmillan is the global academic imprint of the above companies and has companies and representatives throughout the world.

Palgrave® and Macmillan® are registered trademarks in the United States, the United Kingdom, Europe and other countries

ISBN: 978–1–137–34386–4 paperback

This book is printed on paper suitable for recycling and made from fully managed and sustained forest sources. Logging, pulping and manufacturing processes are expected to conform to the environmental regulations of the country of origin.

A catalogue record for this book is available from the British Library.

A catalog record for this book is available from the Library of Congress.

Printed in China.

contents

Series editors' preface   vi

What is time?   1

Rhythm 1: rhythms of the Earth   15

Rhythm 2: rhythms of the body   30

Theatre and memory   43

Clock time   54

Further reading   68

Index   75

series editors' preface

The theatre is everywhere, from entertainment districts to the fringes, from the rituals of government to the ceremony of the courtroom, from the spectacle of the sporting arena to the theatres of war. Across these many forms stretches a theatrical continuum through which cultures both assert and question themselves.

Theatre has been around for thousands of years, and the ways we study it have changed decisively. It's no longer enough to limit our attention to the canon of Western dramatic literature. Theatre has taken its place within a broad spectrum of performance, connecting it with the wider forces of ritual and revolt that thread through so many spheres of human culture. In turn, this has helped make connections across disciplines; over the past fifty years, theatre and performance have been deployed as key metaphors and practices with which to rethink gender, economics, war, language, the fine arts, culture and one's sense of self.

Theatre & is a long series of short books which hopes to capture the restless interdisciplinary energy of theatre and performance. Each book explores connections between theatre and some aspect of the wider world, asking how the theatre might illuminate the world and how the world might illuminate the theatre. Each book is written by a leading theatre scholar and represents the cutting edge of critical thinking in the discipline.

We have been mindful, however, that the philosophical and theoretical complexity of much contemporary academic writing can act as a barrier to a wider readership. A key aim for these books is that they should all be readable in one sitting by anyone with a curiosity about the subject. The books are challenging, pugnacious, visionary sometimes and, above all, clear. We hope you enjoy them.

Jen Harvie and Dan Rebellato

theatre & time

What is time?

The Moscow Art Theatre (MAT) production of *The Seagull* in 1898, directed by Constantin Stanislavski and Vladimir Nemirovich-Danchenko, was a crucial milestone for the fledgling theatre company that has been described as 'one of the greatest events in the history of Russian theatre and one of the greatest new developments in the history of world drama.'

I have drawn the above information from Wikipedia because it was the quickest thing to do, and don't we all operate with deadlines? Avoiding the temptation to add yet more to your stockpile of information, please pause, take a breath, think about the speed at which you plan to consume this short book, and read again more slowly the quotation, noticing

1

how the information has been packaged for us. One past event nests inside three temporal boxes. The production happens within one particular year, within a sequence of events which constitute 'the history of Russian theatre'. (When did that start, by the way? Nothing in Wikipedia, but I have on the shelf a volume conveniently entitled *A History of Russian Theatre*, where the first dated event is a representation of sodomy recorded by a German tourist in 1637.) This brief national history sits inside the bigger box of 'world' theatre history, conventionally dated back to the writings of the ancient Greeks. Time by this standard account is something we are *in*. Can we therefore touch it or see it? *In* or *on*? Notice in my gobbet from Wikipedia the metaphor of the milestone, which pictures time as though we were *on* a road. In practice it is impossible to conceptualise time except through spatial metaphors of this kind. Time flows past us, it reaches out in front of us, we go through it, it runs by too quickly, it is behind us now. Metaphors are always loaded, and the milestone is no exception. We are heading towards somewhere, and counting off the miles to our destination. And that destination is presumably 'now'. So perhaps we should conclude that time is simply a function of our point of view and does not have any existence in itself? The road metaphor entails notions of progress, consistent with the word 'development', and is not compatible, for example, with Buddhist or older European conceptions of time as cyclic, something that continuously repeats itself. If we favoured cyclicity over development, we might prefer to claim that phases of change in theatre alternate with phases of stability in a never-ending quest for the real, and unhook this particular performance event from the ideology of 'progress'.

Instead of placing *The Seagull* in time, we might feel more comfortable discussing it as a play *about* time. It is a drama about the experience of wasted lives, and empty dreams of the future. In Act One a young romantic intellectual stages a playlet exploring the future of the Earth long after the extinction of humankind, and Chekhov seemingly invites us to think how post-Darwinist anxieties relate to the angst of a declining upper class. This kind of analysis is important, but can be made on the basis of the script alone. In this short book I will not be concerned with plays *about* time, or with related questions of historical setting, character development and narrative structure. My concern will be with performance, and the way in which plays are neither *in* time nor *about* time, but are *of* time.

This of-ness is more easily experienced than written about, though Nemirovich-Danchenko did his best in a rapturous letter to Chekhov after the celebrated 1898 performance. 'Not a single word, not a sound was lost. The audience not only got the general atmosphere, or the *plot*, which in this play is so difficult to define, but every thought, everything that makes you the artist and thinker that you are, everything, everything, in short, every psychological movement – everything hit the mark and kept the audience in suspense' (Chekhov and Stanislavsky, *The Seagull*, 1952, p. 70). He is talking, essentially, about time, or timing. Sounds and words and movements struck the audience because the audience was in suspense, attentive, waiting to receive. This shared experience of time, everyone seeing and feeling the same thing at the same moment, is described by Nemirovich-Danchenko as 'atmosphere', and by Stanislavski as 'mood'. Stanislavski tells us in his autobiography that he could not describe to the actors what he wanted here, he could only demonstrate, and as an actor he gave himself up to a 'mood' which he evoked as a cavern holding the treasures of Chekhov's soul (*My Life in Art*, 1980, pp. 352–53). We have somehow to bridge this mystical language to the technical information in his prompt book if we want to understand how he shaped the performance in the medium of time. We read in the prompt book that an initial soundscape evoked the Russian countryside in order to 'help the audience to get the feel of the sad, monotonous life of the characters' (Chekhov and Stanislavsky, *The Seagull*, p. 139). Ten seconds of stillness elapsed after the opening of the curtain, then hammering, then humming, then silent smoking and cracking of nuts before any text was delivered. The production was not unlike a musical composition.

Though he succeeded with *The Seagull*, Stanislavski lamented that he did not possess a similar 'technique for the saying of the artistic truth in the plays of Shakespeare. This is what interferes with our living him over, and forces us to act him, to declaim, to falsify, to pretend, and to achieve nothing' (*My Life in Art*, p. 350). An old-style actress in *The Seagull* declaims a piece of *Hamlet* in precisely this dead fashion. Why did Stanislavski feel that Shakespeare was out of date? Was it a problem of content, or were the time

4

values of translated Shakespearean verse too remote from those of 1898, making that text impossible to share with an audience? To address that question, we might ask ourselves whether the time values of 1898 can be shared with an audience in the early twenty-first century.

Here is how Chekhov's play begins, in a fairly literal translation:

> **Medvedenko:** Why do you always go about in black?
> **Masha:** Because I'm in mourning for my life. I'm unhappy.

A production in London's Southwark Playhouse in 2012 transposed the play to a contemporary setting, a strategy more often applied to Shakespeare. And the dialogue was transposed accordingly (by playwright Anya Reiss):

> **Medvedenko:** Again?
> **Masha:** What?
> **Medvedenko:** Again?
> **Masha:** Black. I'm in mourning.
> **Medvedenko:** For?
> **Masha:** My life.
> **Medvedenko:** Why?
> **Masha:** I'm unhappy.

I have culled this extract from a review by the BBC radio arts pundit Mark Lawson. Lawson comments that Reiss 'has not only stripped the speeches of their facile delivery of back-story but also caught the cagey, resentful, fragmentary nature of much modern inter-generational conversation. ... In the 116 years since *The Seagull* was first staged, audiences, due to TV and film, have become quicker at picking things up, needing to be told less' ('Translating *The Seagull*: How Far Can You Push Chekhov?' *Guardian* online 20 November 2012). A couple of months earlier, a similarly updated production of *Three Sisters* at London's Young Vic transposed the eight sentences of Olga's opening speech into the nineteen shorter sentences required by a contemporary stage idiom. These two productions clearly sought to avoid a modern form of 'declamation', a predictable and rhythmically dead rendition of Chekhovian melancholy. I have no quarrel with Lawson's claim that people today often talk in this fragmentary manner, but I'm wary of the implicit claim that people have become more intelligent, and that the back story ('why do you *always* ...') is inherently facile. I would prefer to say that we live today in a different, faster rhythm, triggered by the speed of modern communications. We are, most of us, too impatient to tolerate a ten-second pause after the curtain rises and before anything happens – unless we know we have committed ourselves to a piece of 'durational theatre'. Because we live at speed, we do not breathe so deeply, short sentences come more easily, and we can more comfortably share the breathing patterns of these twenty-first-century figures who speak in soundbites than the deeper breathing patterns of the late nineteenth century. In modern London everything is illuminated, so we do not have to endure the long darkness of the Russian winter, and understandably we do not have the same patience to endure silence. Many of the things which the Moscow audience noticed on a December night in 1898 we are no longer capable of noticing. When Masha enters cracking nuts, does the rhythm of this activity betoken a pleasure in food which belies a melancholic pose, or does it suggest the nervous symptoms of bulimia? Have we time to care? Our social and working lives are certainly too pressed to allow *The Seagull* to be carved into four acts with three intervals. We live to a different rhythm, and I will have much to say about rhythm in the course of this book.

Mark Lawson celebrates the true-to-life quality of Anya Reiss's dialogue, just like generations of critics and practitioners who ever since Aristotle have claimed that the latest form of theatre represents life in a more 'real' or 'natural' way. What Lawson does not comment on is the rhythmic patterning of Reiss's dialogue, clearly inspired by the dramatic language of Beckett and Pinter. It is the crafting of these lines into two movements that gives them their power. When plays ceased to be written in verse, rhythms did not become any the less important; they just became harder for actors to seize without the aid of a director. An influential adaptation of *Three Sisters* by the Wooster Group in 1991 carved the opening monologue into question-and-answer form. Audiences used to hearing plays by Beckett and Pinter or by the Wooster Group are attuned to the rhythmic subtlety of these lines, and their memories of past performances may trigger their emotional response in the present. This production's supposedly contemporary dialogue is haunted by internalised rhythms that constitute ghosts of the past.

When we try to describe what made the Moscow audience so excited on a December night in 1898, one approach is to say that the actors achieved 'presence', and that actors and audience alike were totally absorbed in the now. A psychological movement like the exhalation of tobacco smoke demanded absolute focus, and left no room for the spectator to think of her last social encounter or for the actor to think about his next line. This descriptive vocabulary is fine until we try to pin down what exactly we mean by 'now' or 'present'. If you isolate a single note of music, it ceases to be music. By the same token, when Medvedenko exhales tobacco smoke, the response of the audience depends on their mood, which involves a remembering of the preceding soundscape, and upon the anticipation that his exhalations will turn into pent-up speech. In other words, they cannot inhabit a 'now' without thinking both backwards in time and forwards in time. And if 'now' strictly does not exist, it becomes problematic to speak of theatre being 'ephemeral' by comparison with forms like painting, poetry and cinema.

At the start of the twentieth century, many modernist artists were influenced by the philosophy of Henri Bergson, who argued that we should uncouple time from space, and seek the pure experience of duration, because space relates to the external world, while time is an aspect of consciousness and self. If we cease to think of time as a thing, but manage to apprehend it as part of ourselves, then we discover the freedom to be ourselves. His ideas were welcomed by those who wanted to use art not to represent reality out there but to express an inner truth. The old form of the 'well-made play', with its three-act structure complicating and then logically resolving a dramatic situation, gave way to less predictable forms that seemed more intuitively to capture the way we think and feel. Notice, for example, how Stanislavski thought of himself as getting inside the mind of Chekhov, and how Nemirovich-Danchenko emphasised atmosphere over plot. Bergson retained his appeal for a generation of French philosophers known as 'phenomenologists', who argued that we should concentrate on how the world actually appears to us, and not rely on some logical analysis of how the world ought to be. Maurice Merleau-Ponty in his *Phenomenology of Perception* (2002; originally published in 1945) followed in Bergson's footsteps when he argued that in order to be a human being, a human subject, one has to *inhabit* and be part of time (pp. 161–62), but he criticised Bergson's separation of mind from body, and argued that we cannot apprehend time through thought but only through our senses. My body is not some object from which I can actually separate my sense of self, and by the same token time is not some thing inside which I exist. Modern research into the neuronal mechanisms of the brain sits comfortably with Merleau-Ponty's insistence that there is no such category as pure thought.

Five years after Merleau-Ponty, Gaston Bachelard, another French phenomenologist, argued in his *Dialectic of Duration* that Bergson was on the wrong track in trying to understand duration as an experience of unbroken continuity. Molecular physics and the study of radiation had taught him that there is movement in all matter, so the separation of time from space was an impossibility. The study of biology revealed that in all forms of life there is dialectic or rhythm, never simple continuity. We cannot live without breathing, and yogic breathing is a good key to human happiness. More broadly, he argued that we can only perceive things in relation to other things: for example, a singer cannot produce a pure musical note without our being aware of something else, a level of intensity or vocal power. A generation later, Bachelard's concept of 'rhythmanalysis' was picked up by Henri Lefebvre, who used it to analyse the rhythms of modern cities – the rhythms that I have related to twenty-first-century versions of Chekhov. Lefebvre contrasted the mechanical rhythms of capitalism with the polyrhythmia of a more natural human life.

While thinkers in the Marxist tradition have never faltered in their determination to place human beings in history, the movement known as post-structuralism is associated with a downgrading of history (i.e. time), and with the prioritisation of space. Thus Michel Foucault proclaimed prophetically in 1967:

> The present epoch will perhaps be above all the epoch of space. We are in the epoch of simultaneity: we are in the epoch of juxtaposition, the epoch of the near and far, of the side-by-side, of the dispersed. We arc at a moment, I believe,

when our experience of the world is less that of a long life developing through time than that of a network that connects points and intersects with its own skein. (Cited in David Wiles, *A Short History of Western Performance Space*, 2003, p. 7)

Foucault's excitement in the face of globalisation and new media is palpable. The post-structuralist mindset liked to think of the past as a set of fragments quoted in and for the present. A live theatre performance was described and analysed as if it was a kind of 'text', and a text is something that exists in space not time. And in the age of 'post-modernity' it became unfashionable to think of theatre as being part of a continuous tradition. Today there has been some swinging back of the pendulum, now that economic models of growth and progress have lost their credibility. As people work faster and faster in an age of instant communications, fighting the constraints and pressures of time has become an almost universal experience. Bergson emphasised our personal experience of time, but today it is perhaps our social experience of time that most requires to be understood.

The first great philosophical meditation upon time was written by St Augustine, who identified in his *Confessions* many of the logical flaws underlying popular accounts. While the pagan Greeks broadly regarded human happiness on earth as the only sensible moral goal, and argued about how to get there, Augustine as a Christian was fixated by a vision of eternal life, and saw theatre as yet another indulgence in the temporary pleasures of the flesh. He tried to look into his own unconscious mind in order to discern another dimension of time. In the first act of *The Seagull*, the idea that some kind of 'world soul' exists over and beyond material reality shapes the play-within-a-play, a visionary drama set 200,000 years in the future, after all forms of organic life have been extinguished. This cosmic and spiritual mode of thought does not appeal to most of Chekhov's protagonists, who are more concerned by the quest of human beings for happiness. Today most of us probably share Chekhov's materialist vision of the world (he was in fact a doctor), but possibilities of a new society seem less promising than they did in pre-revolutionary Russia. We end up discarding not only the idea of an eternal soul but also the idea of a future that justifies the present. Because our spatial horizons have opened up with today's ease of communications, our temporal horizons have to some extent closed down and we are less securely anchored to past and future. In a consumer society, it is hard to escape from conceptualising time as a resource that we want to spend or consume to our maximum possible profit. Time begins to seem like a thing, not a mode of being.

If we contrast Stanislavski's Chekhov with twenty-first-century Chekhov, we shall perhaps understand better today's mode of living time. Stanislavski created a fictive world behind the proscenium of the Moscow Art Theatre, and his naturalistic scenography carried time values with it. The audience of *Three Sisters* in 1901 were taken on an imaginary journey from midday through evening to night and back to midday. The play started in spring, made evident by buds peeping through the windows, and ended in autumn, demonstrated by the steady fall of yellow leaves, which helped set the tempo for the last act. These two rhythms are superimposed on the linear trajectory of the plot, which extends over several years. The audience doubtless responded to this polyrhythmia (Lefebvre's term) because many had returned from summer in the countryside to the Moscow theatre season, which helped them endure the long frozen nights. At the Young Vic, the aesthetic was very different and the audience were conceived as sharing the same space as the stage. There was nothing in the scenography to evoke a sense of time, and thus when Olga opens the play by saying 'Father died exactly a year ago', her words become a statement about the present rather than a statement about the past.

Stanislavski's set was filled with objects, including the mother's clock, which is smashed by her former lover in the third act, and these stage objects reinforce the sense of a past that interacts with the present. The set at the Young Vic aspired to abstraction, and was dominated by an ever-shrinking mound of earth that carried echoes of Beckett. It was a symbol for the audience in the present to interpret. While most of the characters wore twenty-first-century costume, consistent with the coarsened colloquial language and David Bowie's music, the three sisters themselves wore more dated outfits, emphasising Chekhov's white/black/blue colour coding. This sartorial strategy helped to obscure a problem in the update: the plot turns on the impossibility of Masha (the sister dressed in black) ever leaving her husband in order to find happiness with her soldier lover, yet that impossibility is reliant on what we might call the 'Victorian' social values of 1901, not the moral values of 2012. By seeking to transpose the world of the play into 2012, rather than creating a dialogue between past and present, the director, Benedict Andrews, reached an impasse. Perhaps he felt that the Young Vic audience – and note the significance of the theatre's name – were not interested in thinking how the world of a century ago might have shaped the present.

In the third act, when the town is reported to be on fire, the tempo at the Young Vic was set by the stagehands, who steadily removed section after section of the stage, creating an abstract image of loss and containment, whilst reminding the audience of the constructed theatricality of the event in the here and now. In 1901 Stanislavski was preoccupied by the same question of tempo, using rhythm and gesticulation to impress on all the actors the mood evoked by a soul-searing provincial fire alarm. It is unlikely that the intensity of this fire alarm was a simple function of speed. Stanislavski explains how he learnt in rehearsing *Three Sisters* that the audience's experience of a heightened tone and quickened tempo did not relate to the actual speed of verbal delivery (*My Life in Art*, p. 372). Stanislavski's production could not possibly be replicated in the twenty-first century, because the spectator today lives to a different rhythm. The Moscow production was set in the now of 1901, but that historic now also, for example, involved the audience's awareness that Masha pining for love was also the actress married to Chekhov, sick with tuberculosis and far away in Nice. And

Masha in black must have conjured up her namesake in *The Seagull*, again dressed in black and married to a teacher. The moment of 1901 cannot simply be transposed to the present in the way the Young Vic update implies.

According to Aristotle, the now is what holds time together, making past and future time into a continuous whole. What time is not is a succession of indivisible nows (*Physics* iv.13, vi.9). I have argued in this section that it is worth trying to penetrate the mystery of now, because the maker of theatre has to work in the dimension of time. I have suggested that today's culture is preoccupied, more than most, by the pursuit of an indivisible now, detached from past and future time. I have examined a conspicuously now-oriented production in order to highlight some of the contradictions into which one is led by remorseless pursuit of the present moment. In the next section I shall turn to the question of rhythm. To quote Aristotle again, 'time is a measure of change' (iv.12). Time only exists when we measure and count it, and we can only count something that changes according to a regular measure. That counting is not done in the mind but through a living body, and bodies are only alive when they pulsate.

Rhythm 1: rhythms of the Earth

I shall begin with five propositions about rhythm. Perhaps some will appear more obvious than others.

1. Rhythm is movement. Plato described rhythm as 'ordered movement' when he placed dance at the

centre of children's education. Try to envisage music without the muscular action of the musician, and without something – air or a solid object – striking against something else. Try to imagine yourself listening to a rhythm and standing quite motionless. Because rhythm is motion, it is always linked to e-motion or feeling.

2. Rhythm is organic. It never quite coincides with the 'beat' produced by a machine. Instrumentalists can train using a metronome, but they need a human conductor to create rhythm in performance, for we do not apprehend time with the precision of a machine. Our brain processes different sensory inputs at different speeds, so we do not tap our feet in precise alignment with the words we sing, and in a live theatre acoustic our hearing of sound is complicated by reverberation. Our brain prevents us from hearing sounds as rhythmically connected when they are divided by a gap of more than two or three seconds.

3. Rhythm is obsessive. However hard we try to be arrhythmic, we slip into regular periodicity. Try rotating your two arms in different rhythms – very soon there will be a rhythmic connection. Rhythm energises the performance of repetitive tasks: the Greeks used a piper to help them row warships, the Scots once marched into battle with bagpipes, Radio One assists industrial production in the workplace, and joggers jog with earphones. In the same way, rhythm energises and sustains the delivery of dramatic

text. Once we are caught in a rhythm, it is hard to break free.

4. Rhythm is contagious. We instinctively fall into step with each other, or nod in time with the person we are listening to. Dance has long been bound up with courtship. This is a fundamental principle of human bonding and relates to the connection between actors and audience. Which is why Plato wanted dance to be the basis of political education.

5. Rhythm is the basis of artistic form. If we think of art as the imposition of order upon the chaos of observed reality, then we can learn from the Greek understanding that all visual images possess a sense of movement, that is, rhythm. Plato believed human beings had rhythmic skills that animals lack, but the American philosopher John Dewey in 1934 argued from the perspective of evolution that rhythm pre-exists in nature, so the experience of art begins when humans align themselves with those natural rhythms (*Art as Experience*, p. 154).

St Augustine rejected the materialist hypothesis that time is merely a function of planetary movement, citing the triumph of the Israelites in the Old Testament when God helped Joshua clinch a victory by making the Sun stand still. We can tease ourselves with the same question: if the Sun stood still, would time still exist? Can we abstract time so it is not just a function of the material universe? If we put the God hypothesis to one side, what follows? Dewey made

a convenient division between the internal rhythms of the
human body and the macro rhythms of nature which stem
from the rotation of the Moon around the Earth, and the
Earth around the Sun, and the spinning of the Earth upon
its axis. Believing that humans were social before they were
individual, and looked outwards before they looked inwards,
he concluded that in evolutionary terms the rhythms of the
Earth were primary. Dewey's distinction is a convenient
one, and I shall consider the rhythms of the Earth in this
section, leaving the micro rhythms of the body to my next.
We need to remember, however, that the body has internalised the rhythms of the Earth in all sorts of ways.

Take day and night. The circadian rhythms of the body,
which determine our patterns of sleep and digestion, are
familiar to all nightshift workers and users of long-haul East–
West flights. These circadian rhythms are not acquired, but
embedded in our DNA, as they are in the DNA of many forms
of plant and animal life. We feel and function differently in
the morning and in the evening, and these differences are
inflected by age. When a blogger in New York enquired
whether matinee performances of the musical *Sweeney Todd*
would be of lower quality than evening performances,
initial replies were concerned with the risk of too many
children in the audience or the star being replaced by an
understudy. The last contributor responded: 'Same show,
same quality. ... My only problem with the matinee is that
for "dark" shows like Sweeney Todd, I'd prefer to see them
in the evening' (5 July 2006). In other words, the commercial product is the same, but the spectator feels differently

in the evening, and the killings of the demon barber match
her evening feeling. This post terminated the short discussion, because there was no language in the blogosphere,
or indeed the whole Western aesthetic tradition, capable
of developing this debate about the 'quality' of experience.
Yet the Sanskrit *Natya Sastra* – the classic account of Indian
theatre aesthetics – took it for granted that performers need
to seek Rasas (approximating to 'moods') appropriate to the
time of day or night. Zeami in his classic writings on Noh
theatre explains how the yin principle of the night needs
to be balanced by a buoyant yang performance, whilst the
yang principle of the day needs to be balanced by a gentler
yin interpretation (*On the Art of the Nō Drama*, 1984, pp.
19–20). Humans are more attuned to their environment in
this traditional Eastern mode of thought.

Sunday shopping and Sunday working have weakened
the rhythm of the seven-day week, and fewer people regard
theatregoing as just a weekend activity, within the seven-
day cycle of work and rest. Though we increasingly live in
a 24/7 culture, human biology makes the rhythm of day
and night harder to escape than the rhythm of the week.
The seven-day cycle nevertheless dates back to the book
of *Genesis*, and its cultural resilience became evident at the
time of the French Revolution, when the attempt was made
to institute a ten-day week. The decimal principle was
happily accepted for coinage and measurements of length
and weight, but the rhythms of time proved too ingrained.
The revolutionaries renamed and repositioned the months,
but not even they dared to revert from twelve months to the

ten months of the Roman republican calendar. We feel we know in our bones what a month is.

In preindustrial Catholic society, hours and minutes were of little consequence, but people nevertheless inhabited a complex polyrhythmic temporal environment. For millennia, those who sought a divine plan in the universe were mystified by the impossibility of reconciling the rhythm of the Sun to that of the Moon. In the age of electricity, the phases of the Moon are of scant importance, but in earlier times they meant that people could or couldn't leave their homes at night. The Moon was associated with female cycles of fertility, and according to the waxing or waning of the moon people decided when to plant a seed in the ground, or human seed on their wedding night. Early Christianity attached the story of Christ's crucifixion to the cycles of the Moon, while the story of his birth was attached to the cycle of the Sun, which meant that the precise rhythm of the year shifted from one year to the next according to the date of Easter. Biblical readings and the cycle of church ceremonies turned the year into a recurrent epic drama. Mediaeval Christianity attached to the solar calendar local celebrations of saints, and quasi-pagan celebrations like the solstice and St Valentine's. Formal scripted theatre in the mediaeval period was an extension of the richly textured drama of the year, not a product that could be sold and transposed. The French situationist Guy Debord, in his book *Society of the Spectacle*, which helped spark an uprising on the streets of Paris in 1968, condemned the 'pseudo-cyclic time' of a modern society devoted to consuming images. According to his Marxist argument, festivals have lost their authenticity because they have become detached from the underlying realities of production that sustain life. The modern notion of a 'holiday' relates to the bourgeois distinction between work and leisure time, and has ceased to correlate with the old notion of a 'holy day', which divided time into the categories of sacred and secular. Theatre, which used to be of time, part of the texture of sacred time, became a transferable product which could take place at any moment in time when leisure became available.

Debord oversimplifies of course, and the seasons still shape our social lives in many respects. A play seen at the Edinburgh Festival is not the same as a play seen on a Wednesday night after work, because the journey to Edinburgh constitutes a kind of pilgrimage and creates a more intense audience community – although, to be sure, too many plays in sequence may create an experiential blur. Within commercial theatre, the pantomime is a unique survival of seasonal entertainment, and inviting children onstage is part of its strategy to break down the divide between the real time of the audience and the fictional time of the story. In the early modern world, theatrical activity was particularly associated with the Carnival season, which came to an end with the beginning of Lent in February. This made sense because there was less work to do in the fields, and cities were healthier sites for social interaction in cold weather. In the eighteenth century, with better sanitation and the declining influence of religion, the migratory patterns of aristocrats changed, and they returned from hunting on their estates around Christmas or early spring, lingering in town well into the summer. Theatre flourished while the aristocracy were in town, and girls were taken to theatre boxes so they could be put on view for the marriage market. Today, September is more likely to mark the moment when a European theatre announces its 'season', when office workers, students and parliamentarians return from summer holidays abroad. While the renting of West End venues is largely a matter of availability, a company like the RSC in Stratford-upon-Avon remains reliant on the concept of a 'season' because of the migratory patterns of actors and tourists.

Innovative theatre today is largely a function of metropolitan centres populated by a mobile professional elite living an increasingly 24/7 lifestyle, and this is the world rendered most visible by the media. The desire for seasonal celebration nevertheless remains very strong outside the domain in which 'theatre' now operates. In November 2012, on the weekend after Halloween, I found myself in Whitby, the coastal town in Yorkshire where Bram Stoker set his novel *Dracula*. The whole town had been taken over by Goths, visiting their 'bizarre bazaar' and processing up the long steps to the graveyard below the Abbey, where they photographed each other in highly 'theatrical' costumes, each a flamboyant handmade creation. They would be wearing these costumes again in the evening for the concert by Alien Sex Fiend and supporting acts in the Spa Pavilion Theatre. I was struck by the many flowers pinned to the fence overlooking the beach where Dracula's cargo of coffins was supposed to have been washed ashore, with moving tributes to 'my Nan' or some other loved one. The old pagan Day of the Dead, transformed into the Catholic All Souls' Day, migrated to become the US cult of Halloween, at a time of year when the English were more interested in Guy Fawkes; now, in a post-Christian culture, that annual moment devoted to recalling the dead, coinciding with the dying back of the natural world at the end of summer, has migrated back and shows no sign of losing its resilience. There is, however, little correlation between the popular desire for cyclicity exemplified by this Goth Halloween and the modern social phenomenon known as theatre.

By and large theatre is no longer used to shape our sense of the year, and the passage of time. Although some gain pleasure and security from watching the annual comedy written and toured by Alan Ayckbourn, on the whole people are more driven by an insatiable hunger for the new. In the mediaeval world, absorption in the complex cyclicity of the festive year imparted a sense that one was part of a larger structure of death and regeneration, as one followed in the footsteps of ancestors. The Whitby Goth weekend is witness to the same impulse. At the Alien Sex Fiend concert, spectators wore Gothic costume in order to feel they were participating in the event, as they were participating also in the rhythm of human lives punctuated by death. Modern cosmopolitan time is more linear, predicated on the inevitability of progress, not the inevitability of death.

To illustrate the perspective that I have developed on the macro rhythms of time, I will focus in the remainder of this section on Shakespeare's *Twelfth Night*. Shakespeare grew up in the small country town of Stratford, where he was in close touch with the agricultural rhythms of the old Catholic world, but then migrated to the metropolis of London, dominated by the Protestant rhythms of manufacture and trade. He therefore had his feet in two different time-worlds, the first shaped by the polyrhythmic cycle of annual festivals, the second by the disciplined format of the working week. In the first, the hours of work were determined by the Sun; in the second, by the audible parish clock. The text of *Twelfth Night* reflects this tension. The Countess Olivia, though mourning her brother, dallies with a girl dressed as an adolescent boy to whom she feels sexually attracted, when a clock is heard to strike. She responds:

> The clock upbraids me with the waste of time.
> Be not afraid, good youth, I will not have you.
> And yet when wit and youth is come to harvest,
> Your wife is like to reap a proper man.
> There lies your way, due west. (III.i.115–19)

The Protestant rhythms of work construe time as a resource that should not be wasted. However, Olivia's sexual desire drives her to construct time biologically, thinking of the handsome adolescent as a growing crop waiting to be harvested. The significance of the direction west is symbolic, attaching the boy's literal journey across the stage and metaphorical journey through life to the movement of the Sun.

24

Olivia is torn between duty and biology. As an individual in control of her financial future, she needs to use her time profitably, but as the product of a genetic drive to reproduce, she wants to surrender to a different sense of destiny.

The central action of the play is a power struggle between Olivia's steward Malvolio, who is responsible for managing her affairs, and her uncle Toby, who takes advantage of the biological connection to live in her house. Malvolio tries to stop Toby from late-night partying, protesting: 'Is there no respect of place, persons, nor time in you?' To which Toby responds that he does respect perfect 'time' in the songs he has been singing. He and his friends then debate whether Malvolio is essentially a 'Puritan' or merely a 'time-pleaser'. Again this is a clash of time-worlds. The puritanical Malvolio sees daytime as the time to work and make profits, and condemns the waste of resources by revellers who sponge off the wealth of an aristocratic estate. Toby, on the other hand, represents the world of 'cakes and ale', the world of seasonal Catholic celebrations, and the repetitive folk songs which he sings are imbued with cultural memories. Shakespeare's play related to issues that troubled many aristocrats at the end of Queen Elizabeth's reign, struggling to maintain their landed estates and reliant for survival upon intermarriage with London merchant families.

This tension within the text and storyline correlates with a tension that shaped Shakespeare's career as playwright and entrepreneur. Theatres derived their financial profit from box office takings at the public playhouse, where performances were shaped by the rhythms of the working week, but the actors' licence to perform, together with significant cultural capital, derived from their status as servants of the aristocracy, and they gave frequent night-time performances at court and in private residences. In the public playhouse, time was a battleground, as the merchant elite who governed the City of London gradually moved from seeing theatre as a threat to discipline and profit to seeing it as a legitimate commercial enterprise. The battle-grounds were Lent, and more particularly Sunday perform-ance. Sunday was the day when ordinary working people could most easily get to see theatre, so the compromise reached in the 1580s was to allow performance only after the population had emerged from their mandatory church attendance at around 3.30 p.m. This meant that perform-ances would run on into a winter night, when the streets became harder to police, and also meant that people would still skip church in order to get good seats. Recurrent and increasingly successful attempts were made to ban Sunday performance. As audiences were more and more dominated by men of leisure or of no fixed occupation, the start time shifted back towards 2.00 p.m. This timeslot had a con-text in the pattern of social life, as described by the satirist Thomas Nashe in 1592:

> For whereas the afternoon being the idlest time
> of the day, wherein men that are their own mas-
> ters (as gentlemen of the court, the Inns of the
> Court, and the number of captains and soldiers

about London) do wholly bestow themselves upon pleasure, and that pleasure they divide (how virtuously, it skills not) either into gaming, following of harlots, drinking, or seeing a play; is it not then better (since of four extremes all the world cannot keep them but they will choose one) that they should betake them to the least, which is plays? (*Pierce Penniless*)

Nashe goes on to counter the argument that theatre diverts apprentices from their work and impedes trade on the grounds that at this idle time of day the pleasures of theatre are preferable to the alternatives of drunkenness, prostitution, gambling or treason.

Whilst commercial performance was an affair of the afternoon, essentially weekday afternoons by the time of *Twelfth Night*, performance before the aristocracy was an evening affair, with performances finishing well after midnight. Commercial performances tracked the rhythm of the working week, whilst aristocratic performances took place at significant moments in the cycle of the year. Which leads us to the question of the play's title. This was already a mystery for Samuel Pepys, who on Twelfth Night 1663 went to see a performance in the house of the future Catholic King James II. He judged the play to be 'acted well, though it be but a silly play, and not related at all to the name or day'. Nevertheless the play had probably affected him unconsciously when he sat down in the small hours to write his diary, reflecting on how the pleasures of the Christmas season were now at an end and it was time to do his duty, improve his reputation and make money.

The aristocratic audience at the end of Elizabeth's reign was well aware of an allusion that made sense of the title. On Twelfth Night 1601, the aged Elizabeth sat down to watch a play in Whitehall Palace with a glamorous Italian Count called Orsino at her side, and they engaged in a kind of formalised flirtation – and in Shakespeare's play it is a Count called Orsino who tries in vain to woo Olivia. Shakespeare's play was most likely performed at court the following Christmas, recalling this ceremonial playing out of courtship rituals. We do not know what play the Queen and Orsino watched in 1601, though we do know of another quasi-dramatic ritual in which she participated. Since Twelfth Night is 'Epiphany' and commemorates the coming of the three Kings to visit the baby Jesus, the Queen integrated her social position with the texture of the year by giving gifts of gold, frankincense and myrrh to the priest who represented Jesus in a performance that she witnessed in the chapel.

An Elizabethan lawyer recorded that Shakespeare's play was performed on 2 February 1602 at the great Candlemas feast in Middle Temple, one of the Inns of Court where gentlemen and aristocrats came to study the law. While Twelfth Night closed off the short-term celebration of Christmas, Candlemas (commemorating the moment when the Virgin Mary was purified so she could go out into the world again) marked the end of the extended Christmas celebrations. These celebrations were commonly overseen by a Lord of

Misrule, who was elected on Christmas Eve and whose reign ended at Candlemas. At Middle Temple, the Lord of Misrule was called the Prince d'Amour, the Prince of Love, and the games or role-plays that he set up had an appropriately romantic flavour. As host and compère of the greater performance into which the component of Shakespearean entertainment was inserted, he inflected the way the play was viewed – an extended courtly game, marking the end of the festive period, the dismissal of the Lord of Misrule and the re-establishment of secular time.

It is hard to think of 'Shakespeare's play' as a single entity when we set a commercial afternoon performance at the Globe alongside the aristocratic performance at a late-night seasonal banquet. Consider, for example, the climactic scene where Malvolio is told he is mad for thinking it is daylight. In the afternoon performance, it is all too clear that Malvolio is being bullied. In the midnight performance, under flickering candlelight, the imagination could function more freely, and the world of the audience, like the world of the play, belonged to more or less drunken revellers. It is perhaps because Shakespeare wrote for two different time-worlds that his text proved so versatile in subsequent centuries. Today the mediaeval/aristocratic time-world has vanished, while the commercial regime of the public playhouse survives largely unchanged, apart from the shift to evening performance in accordance with changing patterns of work and illuminated streets. The entrepreneurial Shakespeare commemorated by the reconstructed Globe on London's South Bank has become *our* Shakespeare.

Outdoor performances of Shakespeare in parks and gardens remain popular for their sense of seasonality, but remain on the margins of mainstream theatrical activity. In the second half of the twentieth century, it became normal for productions of this play to present Malvolio in a sympathetic light, as a victim. It offends our sense of decency to see a man bullied on account of his social class, as Malvolio appears to be bullied. This contemporary perception of the play relates to our own position as inhabitants of a linear time-world dominated by considerations of democracy and profit, rather than a cyclic time-world dominated by considerations of status, community and death. Like Malvolio, we measure time by the clock, and the rhythms we have incorporated are those of the working week rather than the rotating year.

Rhythm 2: rhythms of the body

Think   of
Pulse   and we
Think   of a
heartbeat,
boom boom
boom boom
boom boom

(Jonathan Burrows,
A Choreographer's Handbook, 2010, p. 131)

We are aware of rhythm before we are born, and babies of only a few months are alert to rhythmic aberrations. Émile Jaques-Dalcroze, an influential teacher of musicianship who collaborated with the scenographer Adolphe Appia in the early twentieth century, argued that children should not begin learning music by eye and ear alone because rhythm should be acquired by the entire muscular system. It is obvious, for example, that the whole body of an orchestral conductor is engaged in interpreting and communicating a score. According to Dalcroze, the child's instinctive sense of time is informed by three core processes. First comes the heartbeat, which operates independently of the will and thus cannot easily be used in teaching; second is the breath, over which we have partial muscular control; and third is the walk, which he saw as the perfect means to divide time into equal portions so as measure it. The movement of the walk quickly communicates itself to the arms and body. Muscles, Dalcroze insisted, 'were made for movement, and rhythm *is* movement. It is impossible to conceive a rhythm without thinking of a body in motion' (*Eurhythmics, Art and Education*, 1930, p. 39).

Many people before Dalcroze had tracked rhythm back to these three sources in the body. One was Joshua Steele, who in 1775 attempted to find a way of encoding speech, hoping that the performance of an actor like David Garrick could be immortalised like the texts of a great writer. Believing that he lived in an age of progress informed by the clock, Steele claimed: 'Though the INSTINCTIVE SENSE of *periodical pulsation* is certainly coeval with our animal frame, yet the invention of the *pendulum* has made the moderns more accurate and expert in divisions of time than those ancients who had no such help' (*An Essay Towards Establishing the Melody and Measure of Speech to Be Expressed and Perpetuated by Peculiar Symbols*, p. 127). He set out to render the performance of a public speaker as a precise musical score, carved into bars or 'cadences'. 'Our breathing, the beating of our pulse, and our movement in walking, make the division of time by pointed and regular *cadences*, familiar and natural to us' (p. 20). Each of these 'cadences', he argued, takes the form of a rise and fall.

Steele set down his own interpretation of how Hamlet's great monologue 'To be, or not to be' should be spoken, arguing that what appears to be the five-beat line of an iambic pentameter (TI TUM TI TUM TI TUM TI TUM TI TUM) normally falls into six or eight units of time or 'cadences', as the actor works variants upon the underlying meter in pursuit of sound patterns that appear classical and heroic. He recognised that his own rendering of the famous speech had an old-fashioned declamatory lilt to it when he eventually went to listen to David Garrick performing the lines. This great actor, he realised, kept the volume more or less constant, reduced changes of pitch to four or five tones and avoided increasing the pace at emotional moments, and by this means maximised audibility. It was on timing that Garrick relied. When Steele had tried to imagine the phrase 'To die, to sleep No more', he himself had slurred the syllables 'die' and 'sleep' for what he imagined to be dramatic vocal effect; Garrick simply kept the sounds precise, while lengthening the 'No' into a long syllable. Steele was able to measure Garrick's pauses: a crotchet follows 'die', a minim and quaver precede 'to', a crotchet follows 'sleep', and a crotchet precedes 'No'.

Likewise in the famous opening line, 'To be, or not to be', everything turns upon the comma (crotchet after 'be', two crotchets before 'or'), and 'not to be' was spoken lightly in a single beat. Steele explains how rapid pronunciation, anything more than about 2½ syllables per second, must be avoided because it 'keeps the audience in a painful attention, which the want of proper pauses increases'. Garrick himself was impressed by Steele's project, with the reservation that the actor's voice is like a violin, a precious instrument that cannot be replicated mechanically (pp. 40–55).

Steele saw the heartbeat as the basis of the human instinct for rhythm. Since we only experience the heartbeat in stillness, he argued, its pulsation informs the way we think; however, it is ultimately the walk of the human biped that provides the basis for poetry and the natural cadences of speech. The core poetic rhythms are the one:two of the normal walk, and the triple rhythm of the man who limps and drags his second foot, a rhythm reflected in dances like the minuet. Steele looked back to the classical practice of describing units of poetic meter as 'feet', and to an idealised Greek world where song, dance and speech converged. The key to timing, Steele concludes, does not lie in the isolated pause, which he likens to 'an empty room in a house, or a vacant house in a street', but in a structure of cadences which are 'the subject both of sense and intellect, independent of any mark on paper' (pp. 155, 127).

Though Steele's system may be too neat, modern science can have no quarrel with his broad thesis that human beings possess 'an instinctive sense and idea of dividing the duration of all sounds and motions, by an equal periodical pulsation'. It parts company, however, when he links the rhythms of organic life to the physics of the pendulum. The heart, for example, is an asymmetrical organ, and its familiar 'lub–dub' rhythm reflects the pushing of blood through separate valves in different chambers, a rhythm that may be further complicated by ectopic or galloping beats. The pendulum can be adjusted to any speed, but human beings physically cannot hear sounds as part of a rhythmic unit when those sounds are more than about two seconds or less than a quarter of a second apart, which is to say beyond the possible timespan of a heartbeat. We do not experience and divide time on the basis of pure mathematics.

The normal heartbeat (60–100 per minute) is slightly slower than a walker's footsteps (about 110 per minute), but together they marry well with Steele's 2½–3 syllables per second, which represents 75–90 beats of iambic pentameter per minute. The beating of our heart and the movements of our limbs are conditioned by our emotions, and the emotional power of verse lies in our intuitive sense of how language connects to the body. The body is an interconnected system, and we are wired to gesticulate in synchrony with the words we speak. Musicians have for centuries spoken of the 'tactus' as the underlying beat we instinctively tap with our hands or feet – the tactile aspect of music. Breath is another bodily function bound up with how we feel, and how we think, and it is through breathing that we join small rhythmic units together in sung or spoken sentences or 'periods'.

Dramatic texts formerly used punctuation in order to divide language into 'periods', telling the actor exactly where to breathe, whilst modern texts punctuate strictly in accordance with grammar, which is to say the logic of thought rather than the logic of time and feeling. In the 'To be, or not to be' soliloquy as printed in the second quarto edition of *Hamlet*, a text largely based on Shakespeare's manuscript, we find a semi-colon after 7½ lines, indicating a very quick in-breath, a more substantive colon after 14 lines and another semi-colon after 20½ lines, and we reach a 'period' or full stop only after 27 lines. The dynamic of the actor's breath is clear, as the sequence of thought works itself through. Modern actors on the whole are not trained to have this lung capacity, and are encouraged to interest themselves in what lies behind the words more than in the temporal substance of the words. Declan Donnellan gives helpful advice to a contemporary Shakespearean actress: 'Modern punctuation follows modern conventions. It is a modern prose convention that we have many short thoughts. But, whatever the convention, we naturally breathe on the thought. The depth of the breath we take is dictated by the stakes. ... Shakespearean verse demands a lot of breath – the stakes are high and the thought is long' (*The Actor and the Target*, 2002, pp. 255–57). It is hard to create a theatre of big emotions and big mental operations when the body is not expanded to its full capacity.

Stanislavski was alert to the fundamental importance of rhythm and tempo in the theatre. He observed how actors in verse drama would fall back on the obvious rhythms of

end-stopped lines, and how opera singers moved in relation to the simple beat of the music, without any attention to inner rhythms reflecting the movement of thought.
Paradoxically, prose drama offered him more scope for
musical creativity. He described speech as a way of fill-
ing time with sounds, sounds that could be broken up and
grouped in rhythmic sections:

> The nature of some sounds, syllables and words
> requires a clipped diction, similar to eighth- and
> sixteenth-notes in music. Alongside this, others
> must be spoken with greater length and weight,
> like whole or half-notes. ... A third kind ... are
> combined into duplets and triplets, etc. In their
> turn these spoken sounds are broken by pauses
> and breaths of varying length. All the resources
> of the spoken word create a continuous, varied
> Tempo-rhythm, and we can use them to develop
> metrical speech, which we need to communi-
> cate verbally both the sublime emotions of trag-
> edy and the lowly joys of comedy in words. If we
> want to create Tempo-rhythm in speech, we not
> only have to divide sounds into groups, we have
> to count the beats and so create *speech bars*. (*An
> Actor's Work: A Student's Diary*, 2008, p. 490)

As an example he breaks up the sentence 'I came here,
waited a long time to no purpose, and left.' Switching from
full and half notes to eighth and sixteenth notes grouped

into bars, he shifts from calm to anxiety. It is rhythm that catches the feeling beneath the words.

One of Stanislavski's most challenging exercises was to demand of an actor that he 'stand in rhythm'. They were working on a play where a humble bookkeeper with only one line to speak needs to prevent his employer from getting on a train, and Stanislavski tried to help the actor find the rhythm of this scene, within which this one-line role was theatrically speaking the most important. He encouraged the actor to imagine himself standing over a mousehole waiting to cosh the mouse when it emerged. This improvisation allowed the actor to find the inner rhythm which communicated his emotion without the use of overt physical signals. Stanislavski went on to demonstrate multiple ways of buying a newspaper in rhythm, in what the actor understood as an étude comparable to those used by a violinist (Vasily Osipovich Toporkov, *Stanislavski in Rehearsal: The Final Years*, 1979, pp. 31–32).

Rhythm is fundamental to the making of theatre because of the innate human propensity to synchronise. When people walk together, they naturally fall into step, and people in successful conversations tend to replicate each other's gestures and speech rhythms. By the same token, audiences fall in with the rhythm of the stage action. The phenomenon of 'timing' refers to the ability of actors to play creatively with this shared rhythm. In respect of comedy, a subtle analysis of timing was undertaken by the great philosopher of time Henri Bergson, in his book *Laughter*, published in 1900. Everything for Bergson came down to the tension between two sorts of time, the mechanical time of a machine and the experienced time of a biological human being. A comic figure has the rhythm of a machine, and is someone 'with whom, to begin with, our mind, or rather our body, sympathises. By this is meant that we put ourselves for a very short time in his place, adopt his gestures, words and actions ...' (p. 186). We subsequently become aware of the mechanical nature of these actions, and laughter is born from that consciousness, shared with other spectators. Bergson proffered three examples of comic rhythms: the Jack-in-the-box, the jumping Jack and the snowball. In each of these there is a tension between *organic* properties – the man-made ball of snow, the lifelike puppets – and the mechanical process by which the Jack-in-the-box suddenly boings upwards, the jumping Jack responds to the pull on his strings, the snowball gathers size and momentum rolling downhill. When human beings behave in this way, they lose what Bergson would later describe as their consciousness of duration, the essence of being alive and endowed with free will. The art of the comic actor lies in finding complex mechanistic rhythms that tantalise the spectator by appearing at first to be organic.

Rhythm is no less important for the production of tears. Edward Gordon Craig, for example, undertook a minute analysis of timing in the work of his mentor, Henry Irving. He explains how Irving tackled Shakespeare in the late nineteenth century:

> He was for ever counting – one, two, three – pause – one, two – a step, another, a halt, a faintest

turn, another step, a word. (Call it a beat, a foot, a step, all is one — I like to use the word 'step.') That constituted one of his dances. Or seated on a chair, at a table — raising a glass, drinking — and then lowering his hand and glass — one, two, three, four — suspense — a slight step with his eyes — five — then a patter of steps — two slow syllables — another step — two more syllables — and a second passage in his dance was done. And so right through the piece — whatever it might be — there was no chance movement; he left no loose ends. All was sharp cut at beginning and end, and all joined by an immensely subtle rhythm — the Shakespearean rhythm ... (*Henry Irving*, 1930, p. 77)

Although Craig claims that Irving learnt his control of rhythm from the complexity of Shakespearean verse, it is clear that Irving constructed his own particular rhythmic patterns melding language, gesture and movement in search of what Stanislavski was also trying to locate, rhythms that express the thoughts and feelings which lie behind what is said.

Seeking to understand how Irving was able to wring the hearts of his audience, Craig analysed his first entrance in the role of Mathias, the guilt-ridden burgomaster in Leopold Lewis's *The Bells*, a role which Irving played repeatedly between 1871 and his death in 1905. Craig examined Irving's arrival so carefully because it was his 'manner of timing the appearance, measuring its speed and direction,

which created a rhythm that was irresistible'. First Craig
had to describe the applause which seemed to be part and
parcel of the performance, something the audience had to
release in order to concentrate. The actor seemed to relax
everything 'while the applause rolls on and up. Twice,
maybe three times, he, as it were, shifts one foot (his right
I think it was), and by this slight and meaningless gesture a
limit is being reckoned to the applause which goes on and
on – no other motion, except that the foot in shifting sends
a slight vibration also without significance, through the
whole person before us – and then as the applause dies away,
at the first sign of it dying, the actor clips it off by a sudden
gesture of awakening from his long and patiently-endured
ordeal'. Irving's foot movements conduct and give shape
to the applause so he can calibrate his performance to the
audience (pp. 54–56). After his opening words, 'It is I! –
It is I!', spoken as two monosyllabic beats over the tail-end
of the applause, Irving inserted into the script four repetitions of 'At last!', the third spoken by Mathias's daughter.
The audience's sense of time – they have been waiting fifteen minutes for Irving to appear 'at last' – converges with
the fictional time of the play, within a shared performance
rhythm.

While listening to news of the mesmerist who might
unmask him as the murderer, Irving slowly removes his
boots. 'It was, in every gesture, every half move, in the
play of his shoulders, legs, head, and arms, mesmeric in the
highest degree – slowly we were drawn to watch every inch
of his work as we are drawn to read and linger on every

syllable of a strangely fine writer.' A poetics of movement blended here with the poetics of text. Craig describes how Irving's hands moved at a snail's pace back up his legs until 'motionless – eyes fixed ahead of him and fixed on us all – there he sat for the space of ten to twelve seconds, which I can assure you, seemed to us all like a lifetime, and then said – and said in a voice deep and overwhelmingly beautiful: "Oh, you were talking of that – were you?" And as the last syllable was uttered, there came afar off the regular throbbing sound of sledge-bells ... I assure you, that time seemed out of joint, and moved as it moves to us who suffer, when we wish it would move on and it does not stir' (pp. 58–60). Through his control of verbal and bodily rhythms, Irving created a sense of artistic beauty, alongside what Bergson called 'duration' – the awareness of time in its passing, a heightened consciousness of being alive.

Critics complained that Irving could not walk properly onstage, but Craig explains how 'something was added to the walk – a consciousness', so the walk constituted a rhythmic language of its own, an artifice that paradoxically flashed 'with the light and the pulse of nature' (pp. 73, 78). In respect of Irving's heartbeat, Craig's mother, Ellen Terry, described how, when Irving as Mathias 'heard the sound of the bells, the throbbing of his heart must nearly have killed him. He used to turn quite white – there was no trick about it. It was imagination acting physically on the body' (Jeffrey Richards, *Sir Henry Irving*, 2005, p. 403). No doubt the hearts of the audience also beat faster in sympathy. As for breath, some claimed that Irving massacred the

English language by jerking out his words in staccato fashion broken up with movements, and avoiding chest resonance. Perhaps it was industrial pollution, or perhaps it was a new sense of the gap between the public facade and the guilty inner man, that caused Irving to breathe differently than actors had breathed before. Irving's control of the complex interface between walk, pulse and breath allowed him, as it were, to carve theatre in the pure dimension of time.

Irving marked both the beginning and the end of an era. He was a modernist who knew how to represent the workings of the unconscious, but he was also one of the last great actor–managers able to use text as raw material for working an audience. Shaw spoke for the new generation of playwrights when he complained how a play was to Irving merely 'a length of stuff necessary to his appearance on the stage, but so entirely subordinate to that consummation that it could be cut to his measure like a roll of cloth' (Richards, *Sir Henry Irving*, p. 313). Theatre in the modernist era would be dominated by the regimes of the playwright and the director, and by the idea that drama was a vehicle for communicating concepts. Irving himself was well aware that he would have destroyed the fabric of Chekhov's *Three Sisters* if he had attempted to act in it (Craig, *Henry Irving*, p. 237). Plays in the twentieth century increasingly became events that took place *in* time, rather than being composed *of* time.

The complaints about Irving's diction exemplify a recurrent principle. Each generation of performers seeks a rhythm of speech that connects to the rhythm and tempo of its audience. Repeatedly a new generation appears and recasts language in a form that is sensed to be more real, closer to the way people actually speak, suppressing the easy tendency to reproduce the way actors have spoken or 'declaimed' before. Garrick, Irving, Beckett, Crimp... however real their language seemed or seems, it is actually poetic, rhythmic, crafted and attuned to the body. Time has a history, and in many respects that history is cyclic.

Theatre and memory

In Aristotle's famous formulation, tragedy is an imitation of an action. This implies an inevitable doubleness. The audience is aware both of the performance in the here-and-now and of the action in some prior place and time that is being imitated. In this sense theatre cannot escape being an act of memory. On a superficial level, actors remember their lines and moves learnt in rehearsal; on a deeper level, all plays are retellings of old stories, and the audience calls back to memory a cultural myth – how Oedipus killed his father, how in a benevolent universe sinners like Mathias always get their comeuppance, or how boy meets girl in the eternal love story. The actors always perform slightly differently, and the story is always told in a slightly new way. Richard Schechner updated the terminology but not the concept when he wrote of 'performance' as a piece of 'restored' or 'twice-behaved' behaviour involving varying degrees of impersonation (*Performance Studies: An Introduction*, 2006, pp. 28–29).

Acting involves the imitation and arousal of emotion, and depends upon remembered emotions, not merely a remembered script. The actor needs to recall either what it felt like to be in a certain situation or how people behave when they are in a certain emotional state. This has led to centuries of debate. Can we remember feelings? Or does the actor need to remember physical actions, to restore strips of behaviour in Schechner's terminology, in order to recreate emotion? Or is emotion in itself a physical action? The word 'emotion' derives, after all, from 'motion', movement. The problem of memory is fundamental.

St Augustine conceived of memory in primarily visual terms, and thought of the human mind as a hall filled with images. Many have followed him in this. Peter Brook, for example, wrote: 'when a performance is over, what remains? Fun can be forgotten, but powerful emotion also disappears and good arguments lose their thread. When emotion and argument are harnessed to a wish from the audience to see more clearly into itself – then something in the mind burns. The event scorches onto the memory an outline, a taste, a trace, a smell – a picture. It is the play's central image that remains ...' (*The Empty Space*, 1968, p. 136). His own remembered images or pictures included the two tramps under a tree in *Waiting for Godot*, and Brecht's Mother Courage hauling her cart with no children to help her. When it came to remembering emotion, Augustine was in no doubt that feeling disappears, and suggested that memory functions like a stomach of the mind. We can bring food up to the mouth again like a ruminating cow, but the grass has lost its taste (*Confessions*, pp. 191–92). We know conceptually how we felt, but not what it felt like to feel that way.

The problem of how the actor remembers emotion was of special concern to Stanislavski, who insisted that actors had to rely on their stock of personal memories and not upon an inherited gestural and vocal code. Like Augustine, he conceived of the memory as a kind of storehouse, and likened the recall of a particular emotion to searching for a bead hidden in a box within a drawer within a cabinet within one room of a particular house (*Actor's Work*, p. 207). Almost impossible. In the first year of his training programme, he encouraged students to try different ruses to recover their beads of personal memory, and to understand how these were bound up with verbal and visual memories. In the second year, he turned to the phenomenon of rhythm as a means of resolving the intractable problem of how to recall emotion. 'Everything you have learnt about Tempo-rhythm leads us to conclude that it is our closest friend and companion because it is frequently the direct, immediate, at times almost automatic stimulus to Emotion Memory and consequently to inner experiencing.' He celebrated as a new discovery his understanding of the effect that 'Tempo-rhythm has on wilful, arbitrary, disobedient and apprehensive feelings, which won't take orders, which shy away at the least hint of being forced and hide away where they can't be got at' (p. 502). Rather than understand emotion in the dimension of space – demarcated by a particular gesture or facial expression – he placed emotion by this means in the dimension of time. In his work on Tempo-rhythms, Stanislavski encouraged actors to find the different tempos for external action and inner feeling, and so, for example, counterpointed the inner turmoil of Chekhov's three sisters against their display of outward calm. Students were taught to use the metronome in order to move between such inner and outer rhythms. The 'method of physical actions' which he refined at the end of his career did not cease to emphasise the rhythms which shaped those actions.

When Stanislavski's system was exported to the United States by Lee Strasberg, the question of rhythm was not on the agenda. It was probing into self that fascinated actors and audiences in the post-war era. And this was also the age of cinema, when audiences were interested in the facial close-up and the immediacy of spectacle rather than the ordering of time. Strasberg's version of emotional memory owed much to Freud's account, according to which repressed memories of traumatic past events need to be released in the present. Thus, he encouraged the actress struggling to play Masha's confession in *Three Sisters* – the scene where the married sister confesses she is in love with a married man – to uncover a repressed childhood memory of confession in church. Indeed, he claimed, it was the actress's repressed memory that had initially caused her to seek out this theatrical role (*A Dream of Passion: The Development of the Method*, 1988, pp. 109–10).

Neither Augustine's account of memory as a storehouse of images nor Freud's account of the unconscious sits comfortably with modern scientific accounts of memory, which envisage multiple networks, patterns or systems connecting up neurons that fire in diverse parts of the brain. There can be no fixed repository of memories when the cells of the body keep replacing themselves. The modern science of memory is in a fluid state, with little consensus on detail beyond the broad principle that memories are dynamic, constantly being remade. The search for integrity of self-hood which underlay American method acting cannot easily be reconciled with the scientific postulate of an 'autobio-graphical self', a self that is built out of memories that inter-act awkwardly with our 'core consciousness', our sensory awareness of the present. (See, for example, the work of the neuroscientist Antonio Damasio.) There is also scien-tific consensus that memory has a set of distinct longevities. For any image to imprint itself, we need a sensory memory lasting for a few hundred milliseconds, and it follows that we cannot ever inhabit the present because our brains need time to process visual input. Memories of words and sounds are dealt with on another side of the brain, and we experi-ence another kind of present, lasting for not much more than two seconds, known as the 'phonological loop', suffi-cient to allow us to hear a complex word, a metrical foot or a bar of music as a single momentary entity. A short-term or 'working' memory allows us to group these units of experi-ence and process tunes or sentences, sometimes rehearsing them again and again so they become part of our long-term memory. Motor memory, in relation to continuous activi-ties like cycling, constitutes one of the most durable modes of memory.

Without a theory of memory, we cannot speak analy-tically about the work done by an actor seeking to achieve 'presence' or the experience of a spectator relishing the sense of a live theatrical encounter. In an influential essay entitled 'The Ontology of Performance: Representation without Reproduction' (1993), Peggy Phelan claimed: 'Performance's only life is in the present. Performance cannot be saved, recorded, documented, or otherwise participate in the circulation of representations *of* representations: once it does so, it becomes something other than performance' (*Unmarked: The Politics of Performance*, p. 146). She insisted on the ephemerality and presentness of performance in a desire to combat the commodification of art by capitalism and the reification of women by the male gaze. Her argument pushed critics to find different ways of accounting for the process of remembering and reproducing that seems so inescapably part of what we experience as 'performance'. Philip Auslander (*Liveness: Performances in a Mediatized Culture*, 1999) rejected what had seemed in the twentieth century an all-too-obvious distinction between live and recorded (or mediatised) performance, while Marvin Carlson (*The Haunted Stage: The Theatre as Memory Machine*, 2001) listened with new respect to actors speaking in the green room about the 'ghosts' that haunt the theatres and performances of the present. On the level of social practice, Joseph Roach (*Cities of the Dead: Circum-Atlantic Performance*, 1996) suggested that cultures reproduce themselves not exactly by repetition but rather by 'surrogation', while Diana Taylor (*The Archive and the Repertoire: Performing Cultural Memory in the Americas*, 2003) adopted the metaphor of the 'archive' to describe how our bodies necessarily reproduce the movements of earlier bodies.

Rebecca Schneider (*Performing Remains: Art and War in Times of Theatrical Reenactment*, 2011) argued that popular re-enactments of Civil War battles constitute collective acts of remembering, and could be a paradigm for performance in the artistic sphere, for performances never simply vanish, she argued, any more than dead bodies on the battlefield dissolve into thin air. This has been a distinctively American debate focused around the broad category of 'performance', whilst European theorists, with a stronger sense of ownership of their own cultural tradition, have given more attention to 'theatre', with its specific technical requirements of re-presentation.

As my case study for this section, I shall focus on a European piece of theatre/performance that has lodged itself in my long-term memory, thanks in part to subsequent conversations and access to written documents such as reviews. *Exquisite Pain*, presented by the company Forced Entertainment (Riverside Studios, London, 2005), is/was an examination of memory, and raises questions relevant to all theatrical performance. Unusually for Forced Entertainment, the performance clung rigorously to a written text. The text by Sophie Calle was a book recording day by day, on the left-hand side of each opening, her memory of a painful phone call in 1986 when her lover broke off their relationship. On each right-hand page of this day-by-day diary, she printed an account which had been sent to her of someone else's exquisite pain. On stage, two actors were placed side by side like the pages of the diary, and voiced Calle's text in a sequence of some eighty-eight repetitions.

The repetition of material within Calle's diary text, and the alternation between this text and the multiple narratives voiced by a single male actor, create an incantatory rhythm that has the inescapable forward momentum of a march while communicating the sense that normality has been abandoned. Like a Buddhist chant, the repetition induces a meditative state and a heightened, potentially ecstatic awareness of inhabiting the present while time passes. At the same time, it offers an overt challenge to the audience by contesting the norms of traditionally crafted plays governed by the logic of cause and effect. In such plays – often referred to as 'Aristotelian drama' because of Aristotle's emphasis on plot structure – the spectator is held in suspense, eager to know what will happen next in the story, so all sense of inhabiting the here and now vanishes. Many spectators at the performance which I witnessed in London found this challenge too great. They could not discern Aristotle's rhythm of beginning, middle and end, and walked out. Their staggered departures created another rhythm, and a different kind of tension or suspense. Aristotle's ideal plot structure was related to the goal of catharsis, whereby release from painful memories can be found in a moment of climax, but this performance was posited on the notion of decay, a concept generally preferred in the modern science of memory.

The rhythm of alternation embraced shifts in the tenses of acting. The house style of Forced Entertainment is a studied and sophisticated casualness that creates a feeling of being in the present, of speaking off-the-cuff without benefit of text, prior rehearsal or theatrical training. The illusion of spontaneity is subtle, though it breaks down occasionally, as for example when the company performs abroad with obligatory surtitles. Against this normative present tense, we witness the past-tense acting of the male performer. It is made clear that he is reading from a text, his own voice is not that of the originating writer, and a hint of ironic humour separates him from the emotions of the writer. Balancing this ironic male voice is the more intense delivery of the actress who reads Calle's recension of her own exquisitely painful memories. Stanislavskian method acting is predominantly future oriented, asking the actor to concentrate on the task or objective ahead that will be accomplished as a result of present action, and putting the audience on tenterhooks about what will happen next in the story. There is an appropriate quality of future-tense acting in the actress's rendition of Calle's pain. These subtle shifts of tense enhance the spectator's sense of witnessing the dynamic and fluid processes of memory. (Notice, incidentally, how my description has slipped into the present tense, since the production lives in the present of my memory.)

In her book, Calle accompanies each of her texts with a photograph. Varied and enigmatic photos accompany the borrowed right-hand texts, but the same fixed photo of a red telephone on a hotel bed illustrates her own record on the left-hand page. The changing photos problematise the authority of the borrowed stories, while the unchanging image of the telephone contrasts with the shifting language that charts Calle's memory. In the work of Forced Entertainment, the sense that we live in a mediatised world where everything can be recorded and preserved lies behind a determination to catch 'nowness' within the medium of live theatre. From one point of view their artistic project belongs specifically to the twenty-first century, but from another point of view their quest is ancient and recurrent: how to escape from embedded memories of how actors have done theatre in the past – rhythmic memories, visual memories, memories archived in the body – in order to achieve a more intimate relationship with the public in the present?

Calle's book is an archive of pain, transformed into a publication of exquisite beauty. For the spectators, the appreciative ones, the performance is not only a thing of beauty but also a collective act of remembering, since Calle makes the autobiographical nature of her text explicit. The performance is a remembering of real pain, but that memory has become a source of pleasure. The question arises whether theatre always constitutes a collective act of remembering. It is striking how many plays offer the audience the spectacle of memory: Oedipus remembers killing his father, a ghost condemns Hamlet to remember, Chekhov's three sisters are trapped by memories of an idyllic Moscow, and in Japanese Noh plays the dead linger as ghosts because they cannot lay their memories to rest. For Strasberg, the therapeutic value of theatre lay in drawing out of the memory 'experiences and emotions, that are otherwise locked and blocked, incapable of being expressed, except under artistic and controlled conditions' (*Dream of Passion*, p. 140). How does the recurrent spectacle of figures on stage engaged in remembering relate to the actual memory work done by an audience?

One of the distinguishing features of theatre is its collective nature. As Eviatar Zerubavel has argued in *Time Maps: Collective Memory and the Shape of the Past* (2003), all communities are essentially 'mnemonic communities', bound together by possessing a shared system of memories. Theatre is a space where, by sharing time with each other, we build up a fund of shared memories. Shakespeare's audience became more English when they spent time generating and sharing memories of how Plantagenet kings warred with each other, historical memories strategically refashioned to configure with Tudor ideals. While some dramatists continue today to write public plays in this vein, contesting public memories of the past, much contemporary theatre prefers to focus on private pain, yielding different mnemonic communities. Certain social groups define themselves by being aficionados of the work of Forced Entertainment, just as certain social groups in the past defined themselves by their privileged knowledge of Greek and Roman culture, or knowledge of what happened in Queen Elizabeth's court. When I share my memory of *Exquisite Pain* with others who saw the play with me, or saw it on another occasion, or who appreciate the work of Forced Entertainment, or of Calle, I bond myself to them, and at the same time I refashion my memory to support that bonding. That bonding turns on a memory of something felt. It turns, therefore, on a recognition that we have both or all suffered comparable moments of pain. We remember we once had that feeling, but we needed to be reminded in the theatre of what that feeling felt like. Though we cannot recover that feeling, we can be reassured that others have felt the same emotions we have felt.

Clock time

Time is a socially produced act of dividing and counting, and time therefore has a history. Calendars and clocks are not simply a way of measuring time; they are a means of imparting a rhythm to life, which is another way of saying a discipline to life. Political power has long been bound up with the control of time. Consider the names we use for the months: Decem-ber should, from its Latin root (*decem* = 'ten'), be the name of the tenth month, but we actually have twelve months, because the added months of July and August recall the first two Roman emperors, Julius Caesar and Augustus, who took control of time and shaped it to what they saw as modern needs. The history of theatre is bound up with the history of time. The Imperial Roman theatre, for example, looks like a clock, planned on a circle with twelve evenly spaced points around the circumference.

Greek theatre was embedded in a particular social construction of time. Athenian tragedies were performed during the Festival of Dionysus, celebrated at a time of full moon, whilst the political system was organised around the solar calendar and a division of the year into ten equal months, with a new Council taking its seats every month. Twelve is the cosmic number – there are roughly twelve lunar months per solar year – while ten is the human number – ten fingers, ten toes. There was no rhythm of the working week in ancient Athens, only the intersection of two incompatible calendars. Greek tragedies demonstrated the irreconcilability of the nocturnal religious domain with the manmade sun-lit political domain. They were also embedded in other aspects of social time. Dramatists regularly allocated long speeches of roughly equal length to two speakers arguing against each other, a convention which reflects the technology of the water clock used in the law court to ensure equal opportunity to impress the jury. The dancing of the chorus required an extraordinary level of synchronisation, with text and movement both subject to the same complex rhythms; and when young men learnt to synchronise in this way, they learnt also to think together and fight together as part of a democratic community. Aristotle recognised that the unity of tragic plots was linked to a compression of time, and that the best plays contained their story within the span of one day – though his phraseology actually refers to 'a circuit of the sun' because time was not yet an abstraction but an extension of space. This was the perfect dramatic structure for an audience to gauge the cause and effect of human action, and became normative in the later evolution of theatre. The theory of the three unities of time, place and action helped push the world of the gods and the cosmos to the margins.

Weeks, hours and minutes were almost unknown to the Greeks. Weeks can be related to phases of the Moon, but hours and minutes are purely human constructions. Christianity brought with it the concept of the working week, demarcated by the Lord's day of rest, equivalent to the Jewish Sabbath. Clocks on parish churches made the hour part of how people lived and experienced time, the chiming of the clock serving to organise industrial workshops and the locking of town gates in an efficient and economically productive manner. Marlowe's *Doctor Faustus* (*c*.1592) illustrates the new regime of the clock. In this play, Faustus sells his soul to the devil in exchange for twenty-four years of wish fulfilment on Earth, and in the climactic final scene the audience share his experience of the final hour of these twenty-four years. The play is modelled on mediaeval dramas which charted the span of a single human life en route to salvation or damnation, taking no interest in the classical unities, or in Aristotle's related principle that plays need a beginning, middle and end. But Marlowe's story is packaged for the commercial and professionalised Elizabethan theatre, which had been functioning for barely fifteen years, part of a new leisure industry offering multiple choices to the consumer with money in his or her pocket. Faustus's attempts to live in the present, pursuing science, money, sex and practical jokes played on the Pope, seem increasingly futile as the play goes on. The striking of the clock at the eleventh hour marks, in Marlowe's play, the convergence of two configurations of time: Catholic time, which concentrates on the rhythm of life and death and on the insignificance of life before eternity, and Protestant time, which demands that time be used profitably, filled with good works. Faustus pleads desperately for the heavens to stand still, and evokes other time systems that might prove less cruel – pagan astrology and the Pythagorean (or Hindu) belief that souls transmigrate. The force of his monologue rests upon a tension in the Elizabethan stage: on the one hand, a model of the former Catholic cosmos with a heavenly canopy above and Hell beneath the floor, and on the other hand, an empty space which offers man nowhere to escape and where reality is but the product of human imagination. The second half of Faustus's final hour occupies significantly less stage time than the first half-hour, creating the illusion of time accelerating, and compounding the illusion that twenty-four years have passed in barely two hours of stage time.

There is a significant mismatch in the balance of these two half-hours between 'real' or clock time and the human experience of time. The experience of Faustus anticipates that of many beneficiaries of consumer society, able to take advantage of so many opportunities that they feel bereft of time because time is finite. They sense themselves to be cash rich but time poor. As the German sociologist Hartmut Rosa puts it:

> To taste life in all its heights and depths and in its full complexity becomes a central aspiration of modern man. ... Acceleration serves as a strategy to erase the difference between the time of the world and the time of our life. The eudaimonistic promise of modern acceleration thus appears to be a functional equivalent to religious ideas of eternity or eternal life, and the acceleration of the pace of life represents the modern answer to the problem of finitude and death. ('Social

Acceleration: Ethical and Political Consequences
of a Desynchronized High-Speed Society', 2009,
p. 91)

The progressive acceleration of time can be traced back to
the sixteenth century, and the regime of the clock, which
chopped time first into hours, then subsequently into
minutes, then into seconds. The more it generated measur-
able units of time, the more clock time created a mismatch
between the quantitative and qualitative experience of
time.

The creation of minutes and seconds led to the illusion
that there was such a thing as 'absolute time', a virtual clock
that existed outside and beyond the realm of human beings.
For people like Isaac Newton, this was an important theoretical construct that allowed the advance of science. The
emergence of absolute time correlated with the triumph of
absolute monarchy in Europe, reinforcing the perception of
eternal power structures which human beings can neither
influence nor function without. When the French revolutionaries wanted to return power to ordinary people, they
tried in vain to take control of time and reinstate the decimal principle that references the human body, not religious
tradition. The polyrhythmic human organism does not take
easily to simple mathematical quantification. What the revolutionaries could not achieve by legislation, the mechanical harvester, the industrial loom, the steam locomotive
achieved through the power of economics: subordination of
the body to the rationality of number.

Irving's *The Bells* is a product of Victorian capitalism, a concentrated entertainment designed to be enjoyed after supper by working people who needed to be up again the next morning. Craig recalls how the prompter sat in his corner furnished with a clock and a minute book, recording exactly when the curtain rose and fell, meanwhile baking potatoes on the hot pipe (*Henry Irving*, p. 165). The first act ran for twenty-four minutes, followed by an eight-minute interval; the second twenty-eight minutes, followed by a mere six-minute interval; the third act was longest, at thirty-five minutes, but was broken into three scenes in order to create the sense of time accelerating as Mathias moved towards death. In many respects the play is a rewrite of *Faustus*, concentrating on the hour between eleven and midnight that culminates in Mathias's damnation – for it was upon the stroke of midnight on Christmas Eve that Mathias murdered the Polish Jew. The great dramaturgical change, distinguishing modernity from the age of Marlowe, was to take the audience into the present of the hero's memory rather than accompany the hero in his epic journey along the road of time. In the new format it becomes possible to contrast Mathias's respectable outer world, measured by the clock, with his inner world, bombarded by the bells of the Jew's sleigh. Such a tension between inner and outer rhythms fascinated Stanislavski, inspiring his use of the metronome. In *The Bells*, it is the church bell which defines the rhythm of the external world, a rhythm which includes funereal tolling and wedding chimes that counterpoint Mathias's death scene. While the church bells ring from a fixed point in space, the sound of the sleigh bells moves across the stage, suggesting the elusive nature of consciousness and a mysterious linkage of space to time. The deeper rhythms of the Christian story (the birth of Christ, the death of the Jew, hopes of being saved by a virtuous man called Christian) continue to resonate in this play on the eve of the modernist era.

The cultural geographer David Harvey describes 'time-space compression' as a characteristic feature of life and art in the modernist and post-modernist era. He coined this phrase to depict a set of historical processes 'that so revolutionise the objective qualities of space and time that we are forced to alter, sometimes in quite radical ways, how we represent the world to ourselves' (*The Condition of Postmodernity*, 1990, p. 240). The ever increasing speed of trains, jet aircraft and digital telecommunications, he argues, means that capitalism puts a premium on ephemerality, and if the present is volatile and subject to instant change, there can be no point in engaging with the past or in long-term planning for the future. In a similar vein, Zygmunt Bauman describes how economic power now lies with those who have access to instantaneity, within what he dubs 'liquid modernity'. Throughout human history, he laments, 'the work of culture consisted in sifting and segmenting hard kernels of perpetuity out of transient human lives and fleeting human actions, in conjuring up duration out of transience, continuity out of discontinuity, and in transcending thereby the limits of human mortality' (*Liquid Modernity*, 2000, p. 126). The modern debate about theatrical presence is rooted in reluctance to *perpetuate* a theatrical canon, to *continue* in the footsteps of great actors or to seek out *durable* dramatic writing. In the world of instantaneity, kernels of perpetuity no longer merit a place.

According to Harvey, one common response to the post-modern condition is 'to try and ride the tiger of time-space compression through construction of a language and an imagery that can mirror and hopefully command it' (*Condition of Postmodernity*, p. 351). I shall examine, as an exemplary project seeking to engage with contemporary time, Graham Vick's production of *Mittwoch aus Licht* by Karlheinz Stockhausen, a world premiere presented in a disused chemical factory in Birmingham in 2012. As a maker of theatre, Stockhausen worked in the tradition of Dada and was inspired by his collaboration with John Cage, who was an exponent of the Happening, an American movement in the 1950s that sought to create events which had no meaning beyond their eventness and immediacy. However, he was no less influenced by an esoteric tradition that had its roots in the Middle Ages. *Mittwoch* means 'Wednesday', and Stockhausen's work explored the experiential meaning of that day, a midweek point of convergence. The symbolism of the week related to ancient gods, and to the seven pre-Copernican 'planets', supposed to move at speeds set in a perfect ratio equivalent to a perfect musical scale. In this mode of thought, which goes back to Pythagoras, time and space constitute a single principle within the order of the cosmos. Inspired by particle physics, Stockhausen was happy to throw out materialist interpretations of the world as solid matter, and conceive of the universe as a set of vibrations.

In the first instance, we can think of *Mittwoch* (written 1993–97) as a piece of durational theatre, a fragment of the complete cycle of seven 'days'. The cycle is called *Licht* ('light'), and demands over forty hours of musical playing time. In accordance with the scale of the work, there is no Aristotelian logic of beginning, middle and end, and the four acts of *Mittwoch* have no direct narrative link. Hans-Thies Lehmann explains how the contemporary 'durational aesthetic' prolongs time in order to create a kind of time sculpture, a work made in the dimension of time, drawing on the device of repetition, and countering the tendency of Aristotelian theatre to erase our experience of 'time as time'. Stockhausen constantly remixes and repeats musical elements, in music as in narrative refusing any sense of development and resolution. Vick's production of *Mittwoch* commenced at 4.15 p.m., and could not be viewed at the end of a working day, requiring therefore a different emotional commitment from the audience. The journey to the factory was part of the total experience of time as duration.

Stockhausen's understanding of duration and tempo went further, however. He wrote in 1971 that people's sense of what is fast and slow was traditionally determined by the limits of the human body – breathing, heartbeat and for musicians the speed at which fingers, tongue or lips can move – but that the speed of cars and aircraft had changed our perception of relative speed:

Take timing: when I have to pass quickly through the continuum of speeds and tempi in music, I change completely, and am no longer comparable to someone who is fixed in his time perspective of metronome 70, his heartbeat, or metronome 20 or 30, his breathing, for whom everything that is faster is fast, and everything that is slower, slow. What we need, and what we will become as individuals — some of us — are beings who are able to change their speed and direction of response very quickly, experience all these transformations, and yes, become the sounds. (*Stockhausen on Music: Lectures and Interviews*, 1989, p. 99)

The technology of electronic music gave him the opportunity to transcend the limits of the human body. If you speed up rhythm beyond a certain point, then it is perceived as pitch, and if you slow it down beyond a certain point, then it is perceived as timbre. The common sense that is grounded in our organs of perception can be transformed to offer a different way of knowing the world. At the start of *Mittwoch*, for example, we hear a recording of Stockhausen's own voice uttering the phrase 'Wednesday Greeting', slowed down in order to force us to separate the grain of the voice from any perception of semantic meaning.

The most celebrated — or notorious — section of *Mittwoch* is the string quartet played from four helicopters. Four players of classical instruments compete with, but also try to converge with, the noise that is also a form of music emanating from the rotor blades of the helicopters. The musicians are forced to make themselves at one with the rhythms of the modern world as defined by its means of transport. For the audience, this piece exemplifies a standard trope in post-modern performance: the use of live transmission to create simultaneity, and break up our sense that we possess a single self capable of grasping what the world is really like. The audience meets the players and pilots, watches the live work of the sound designer while following the progress of the musicians on a monitor as they take off, play and land, and then questions them upon their return. We have seen the helicopters flying above the theatre before the event starts, so we know logically that we are participating in a live event, but inhabiting the present of the performance nevertheless feels like an act of faith.

Mittwoch was time-specific in that it coincided with the London Olympics, and received funding for that reason. Stockhausen conceived Wednesday as the midweek point of coming together, and the first act represents a world parliament seeking to create world harmony. Professional *a cappella* singers were mixed with members of the Birmingham community and arranged in a huge circle surrounding the audience, and the text used sounds to create the illusion of foreign languages. The attempt to create musical convergence in the space was complicated by the physical speed of sound, with different voices necessarily reaching different spectators at different times, and the conductor/president used a bell or a gavel rather than a visual gesture in an attempt to create order. In a powerful metaphor, the political problem of creating world harmony became a problem of making time and space converge. From a cosmic perspective, time ceased to be an abstraction and collapsed back into space.

The performance was inspired by the aesthetic ideal of the 'Happening' — a term first coined by the performance artist Allan Kaprow in 1957. The first act, for example, is interrupted by a janitor who leads out the conductor/president because his car is illegally parked, and it is unclear whether this car belongs to the actor or the character. The energetic presence of Graham Vick shepherding the audience contributed to the sense of live event. Yet it was also the performance of a classic text, and a homage to the composer, remembered by the prominent display of his photograph. Not so clear was the relationship between the world of 2012 and the time of the work, written nearly twenty years previously and reflecting a philosophy grounded in the 1960s. There is no place for historical time in Stockhausen's universe, and the encounter with time is inner rather than social, for it is one's inner being that needs to sense the vibrations of the machine and of the cosmos. Stockhausen's basic aesthetic principle was to start by interrogating the present moment, the qualitative experience of the note or noise, and move from there into the discovery of a past and a future. The idea that time is constructed socially and politically was not part of Stockhausen's worldview.

Stockhausen nevertheless points up the major questions that I have explored in this book. He works from the premise that the body does not exist in time, but time is *in* and *of* the body, and he raises the question of how we can reconcile our phenomenal knowledge of time (how it appears to our senses) with our intellectual knowledge that this phenomenal knowledge is false. He was of course primarily a musician, and his exploitation of electronic music obliges us to ask: can the medium of theatre also take leave of direct bodily expression, or does theatre then cease to be theatre? His engagement with technology leads us back to Lefebvre's concept of 'rhythmanalysis', and makes us think how theatre might attune itself to the underlying rhythms of twenty-first-century society. His rigorous quest for the texture of the present moment forces him back to a probing of cultural tradition – in this case, all that defines Wednesdayness. His quest for the nature of rhythm and its roots in the body leads us to think more carefully about the way theatre is grounded in rhythm, and about the ability of rhythm to join human beings whilst spectacle and the gaze tend to separate.

Stockhausen collapses the dichotomy of time and space by spatialising sound, in a practice that we could relate to the theatrical dichotomies of text and performance, voice and movement, sound and meaning which shape contemporary practice. At the start of the twentieth century, Bergson proposed a separation of time from space, seeking for the integrity of consciousness. Einstein rejected this distinction, along with the distinction between past, present and future, in a manner consistent with the mid-twentieth-century ideological assumption that every individual's point of view is equally valid, and that we should not worry ourselves too much about the past and the future. Lee Smolin is a controversial twenty-first-century physicist who wants to throw out Einstein's premise and argue that time is absolute, not subject to evolving laws of nature. Whether or not Smolin's theory makes a lasting impact on scientific thought, it is clear that no scientific hypothesis lasts for ever, and that in the twenty-first century excessive attention to the present is unhelpful for the future of the human race. Does theatre matter in the world of today? To recover time in the theatre is, according to the argument that I have developed in this book, one means, and a very important means, of engaging afresh with the world that we inhabit and are inextricably part of.

further reading

Time is a vast topic, and what follows can only be a selection. Much has been published on dramatic time, which is to say, on the way playwrights organise their narratives – but my concern in this book has been theatrical time, and there is a conspicuous lack of broad-based books on time as the core of theatrical performance. Stanislavski's account of tempo-rhythm in *An Actor's Work* (2008, in sections formerly published under the title *Creating a Role*) remains unsurpassed as a guide to practice. There is a large specialist literature on Shakespearean verse speaking, and Peter Hall's chapter on 'Shakespeare's Verse' in *Exposed by the Mask* (2000) is a good starting point for the uninitiated. Writing from the perspective of dance, Janet Goodridge in *Rhythm and Timing of Movement in Performance: Drama, Dance and Ceremony* (1999) vanishes too much into anthropology for my taste, but I find Jonathan Burrows' *A Choreographer's Handbook* (2010) an inspiration and delight. One needs to turn to musicians for a more theorised analysis of performance time. Eric Clarke's essay 'Rhythm and Timing in Music' (1999), David Epstein's *Shaping Time: Music, the Brain, and Performance* (1995) and Justin London's *Hearing in Time: Psychological Aspects of Musical Meter* (2004) are, at least in part, accessible to the non-musician.

There is a substantial and readable literature on the sociology of time, and the sociologist Barbara Adam offers a good theoretical overview in *Time* (2004). The time-world of contemporary society is examined in Zygmunt Bauman's *Liquid Modernity* (2000), David Harvey's *The Condition of Postmodernity* (1990) and Helga Nowotny's *Time: The Modern and Postmodern Experience* (1994). Time is a construction of human beings, and thus has a history, important aspects of which are explored by Norbert Elias in *Time: An Essay* (1992), Stephen Kern in *The Culture of Time and Space, 1880–1918* (2003) and Donald Wilcox in *The Measure of Times Past: Pre-Newtonian Chronologies and the Rhetoric of Relative Time* (1987). Eviatar Zerubavel, in *Time Maps: Collective Memory and the Shape of the Past* (2003), looks at the present cultural act of shaping time. For the individual act of remembering, we turn to the psychological literature, and you can get a sense of the field by dipping into the essays in Elizabeth and Robert Bjork's *Memory* (1996). For a more entertaining read, try Joshua Foer, *Moonwalking with Einstein: The Art and Science of Remembering Everything* (2011). G. J. Whitrow's *What Is Time?* is a classic and accessible introduction to the history of scientific understandings of time, republished in 2003.

Addressing the philosophical question of what time is, Henri Bergson influentially isolated time from space, and anchored it to individual consciousness. You could start with his account of duration in *An Introduction to Metaphysics* (1912, pp. 9–24) or the opening pages of *Creative Evolution* (1998). Bergson's essay on 'Laughter' (1956) is a thought-provoking introduction to comic timing. Maurice Merleau-Ponty's account of how we experience time through our different senses is most easily approached through lectures published as *The World of Perception* (2004). George Lakoff and Mark Johnson, in *Philosophy in the Flesh* (1999), explore the language we have to use in order to talk about and thus conceive time.

The contemporary quest to create presence and duration in experimental performance is discussed in many books, including Philip Auslander's *Liveness: Performance in a Mediatized Culture* (1999), Hans-Thies Lehmann's *Postdramatic Theatre* (2006) and Rebecca Schneider's *Performing Remains: Art and War in Times of Theatrical Reenactment* (2011). There is no space here for a bibliography covering the many forms – like real-time naturalism, Happenings, verbatim theatre or reminiscence theatre – that play upon the spectator's sense of lived time.

Adam, Barbara. *Timewatch: The Social Analysis of Time*. Cambridge: Polity, 1995.
———. *Time*. Cambridge: Polity, 2004.
Augustine. *Confessions*. Trans. Henry Chadwick. Oxford: Oxford UP, 1991.
Auslander, Philip. *Liveness: Performance in a Mediatized Culture*. London: Routledge, 1999.

Bachelard, Gaston. *The Dialectic of Duration*. [1950]. Trans. Mary
    McAllester Jones. Manchester: Clinamen, 2000.
Bauman, Zygmunt. *Liquid Modernity*. Cambridge: Polity, 2000.
Bergson, Henri. *Creative Evolution*. [1907]. New York: Dover, 1998.
————. *An Introduction to Metaphysics*. [1903]. Trans. T. E. Hulme.
    London: Putnam, 1912.
————. 'Laughter'. [1900]. *Comedy*. Ed. Wylie Sypher. New York:
    Doubleday, 1956. 61–190.
Bjork, Elizabeth Ligon, and Robert A. Bjork, eds. *Memory*. London:
    Academic Press, 1996.
Brook, Peter. *The Empty Space*. London: MacGibbon & Kee, 1968.
Burrows, Jonathan. *A Choreographer's Handbook*. London: Routledge,
    2010.
Carlson, Marvin A. *The Haunted Stage: The Theatre as Memory Machine*.
    Ann Arbor: U of Michigan P, 2001.
Chekhov, Anton, and Konstantin Stanislavsky. *The Seagull*. London:
    D. Dobson, 1952.
Clarke, Eric. 'Rhythm and Timing in Music'. *The Psychology of Music*.
    Ed. Diana Deutsch. New York: Academic Press, 1999. 473–500.
Craig, Edward Gordon. *Henry Irving*. London: Dent, 1930.
Damasio, Antonio. *The Feeling of What Happens*. New York: Harcourt
    Brace, 1999.
Debord, Guy. *Society of the Spectacle*. [1967]. Trans. Donald Nicholson-
    Smith. New York: Zone, 1994.
Dewey, John. *Art as Experience*. London: Allen & Unwin, 1934.
Donnellan, Declan. *The Actor and the Target*. London: Nick Hern, 2002.
Elias, Norbert. *Time: An Essay*. Oxford: Blackwell, 1992.
Epstein, David. *Shaping Time: Music, the Brain, and Performance*.
    New York: Prentice Hall, 1995.
Foer, Joshua. *Moonwalking with Einstein: The Art and Science of
    Remembering Everything*. London: Penguin, 2011.
Foster, Russell G., and Leon Kreitzman. *Rhythms of Life: The Biological
    Clocks Which Control Every Living Thing*. London: Profile, 2004.
Goodridge, Janet. *Rhythm and Timing of Movement in Performance: Drama,
    Dance and Ceremony*. London: Jessica Kingsley, 1999.
Hall, Peter. *Exposed by the Mask*. London: Oberon, 2000.
Harvey, David. *The Condition of Postmodernity*. Oxford: Blackwell, 1990.

Hotson, Leslie. *The First Night of 'Twelfth Night'*. London: Hart-Davis, 1954.

Jaques-Dalcroze, Émile. *Eurhythmics, Art and Education*. Trans. Frederick Rothwell. London: Chatto & Windus, 1930.

Kern, Stephen. *The Culture of Time and Space, 1880–1918*. Cambridge, MA: Harvard UP, 2003.

Lakoff, George, and Mark Johnson. *Philosophy in the Flesh*. New York: Basic Books, 1999.

Lefebvre, Henri. *Rhythmanalysis: Space, Time, and Everyday Life*. Trans. Stuart Elden and Gerald Moore. London: Continuum, 2004.

Lehmann, Hans-Thies. *Postdramatic Theatre*. Trans. Karen Jürs-Munby. London: Routledge, 2006.

London, Justin. *Hearing in Time: Psychological Aspects of Musical Meter*. Oxford: Oxford UP, 2004.

Merleau-Ponty, Maurice. *Phenomenology of Perception*. [1945]. Trans. Colin Smith. London: Routledge, 2002.

———. *The World of Perception*. [1948]. Trans. Oliver Davis. London: Routledge, 2004.

Nowotny, Helga. *Time: The Modern and Postmodern Experience*. Cambridge: Polity, 1994.

Phelan, Peggy. 'The Ontology of Performance: Representation without Reproduction'. *Unmarked: The Politics of Performance*. London: Routledge, 1993. 146–66.

Richards, Jeffrey. *Sir Henry Irving: A Victorian Actor and His World*. London: Hambledon & London, 2005.

Roach, Joseph R. *Cities of the Dead: Circum-Atlantic Performance*. New York: Columbia UP, 1996.

Rosa, Hartmut. 'Social Acceleration: Ethical and Political Consequences of a Desynchronised High-Speed Society'. *High-Speed Society: Social Acceleration, Power, and Modernity*. Ed. Rosa Hartmut and William E. Scheuerman. University Park: Pennsylvania State UP, 2009. 77–111.

Schechner, Richard. *Performance Studies: An Introduction*. 2nd ed. London: Routledge, 2006.

———. *Performing Remains: Art and War in Times of Theatrical Reenactment*. London: Routledge, 2011.

Schneider, Rebecca. *Performing Remains: Art and War in Times of Theatrical Reenactment*. New York: Routledge, 2011.

Smolin, Lee. *Time Reborn: From the Crisis in Physics to the Future of the Universe*. New York: Houghton Mifflin Harcourt, 2013.

Stanislavski, Konstantin. *An Actor's Work: A Student's Diary*. Trans. Jean Benedetti. London: Routledge, 2008.

————. *My Life in Art*. [1924]. Trans. J. J. Robbins. London: Eyre Methuen, 1980.

Steele, Joshua. *An Essay Towards Establishing the Melody and Measure of Speech to Be Expressed and Perpetuated by Peculiar Symbols*. London: J. Almon, 1775.

Stockhausen, Karlheinz. *Stockhausen on Music: Lectures and Interviews*. Ed. Robin Maconie. London: Boyars, 1989.

Strasberg, Lee. *A Dream of Passion: The Development of the Method*. London: Bloomsbury, 1988.

Taylor, Diana. *The Archive and the Repertoire: Performing Cultural Memory in the Americas*. Durham, NC: Duke UP, 2003.

Toporkov, Vasily Osipovich. *Stanislavski in Rehearsal: The Final Years*. New York: Theatre Arts, 1979.

Whitrow, G. J. *What Is Time? The Classic Account of the Nature of Time*. [1972]. Ed. J. T. Fraser. Oxford: Oxford UP, 2003.

Wilcox, Donald J. *The Measure of Times Past: Pre-Newtonian Chronologies and the Rhetoric of Relative Time*. Chicago, IL: U of Chicago P, 1987.

Wiles, David. *A Short History of Western Performance Space*. Cambridge: Cambridge UP, 2003.

Zeami. *On the Art of the Nō Drama*. Trans. J. Thomas Rimer and Yamazaki Masakazu. Princeton, NJ: Princeton UP, 1984.

Zerubavel, Eviatar. *Time Maps: Collective Memory and the Shape of the Past*. Chicago, IL: U of Chicago P, 2003.

index

absolute time, 58
Aristotle (384–322 BCE), 15, 43, 50, 55, 62
Augustine, Saint (354–430), 11, 17, 44
Auslander, Philip, 48
Ayckbourn, Alan (1939–), 23

Bachelard, Gaston (1884–1962), 9–10
Bauman, Zygmunt (1925–), 60
Bergson, Henri (1859–1941), 8–9, 37, 66
body and time, 58, 66
breath, 10, 31, 34, 35, 41–42, 62
Brook, Peter (1925–), 44
Burrows, Jonathan (1960–), 30

Cage, John (1912–92), 61
Calle, Sophie (1953   ), 49–52
Carlson, Marvin, 48
carnival, 21

Chekhov, Anton (1860–1904)
    The Seagull, 3–6, 12
    Three Sisters, 6–8, 12–15, 46
Christmas, 28
clocks, 24, 31
    church bell, 55, 59
    water clock, 55
comedy, 38
consumer society, 12, 20, 57
court theatre, 27–28
Craig, Edward Gordon (1872–1966), 38–41, 59

Dalcroze, Émile, *see* Jaques-Dalcroze, Émile
Damasio, Antonio (1944–), 47
Debord, Guy (1931–94), 20
decimalisation of time, 54, 58
declamation, 6, 32
Dewey, John (1859–1952), 17–18
Donnellan, Declan (1953–), 35
Dracula, 22

dramatic structure, 9, 50, 55, 62
duration, 41
durational theatre, 6, 62

Einstein, Albert (1879–1955), 66–67
emotion, 16, 34, 37, 39
emotional memory, 43–46, 52–54

Forced Entertainment, 49–52
Foucault, Michel (1926–84), 10
French Revolution, 19, 58
Freud, Sigmund (1856–1939), 46

gait, *see* walking
Garrick, David (1717–79), 32–33
globalisation, 11
Greek theatre, 54–55

Halloween, 23
Happening, 65
Harvey, David (1935–), 60
heartbeat, 30–31, 33, 34, 62–63
historical time, 65
holiday, 21

Irving, Henry (1838–1905), 38–42, 59

Jaques-Dalcroze, Émile (1865–1950), 30–31

Lawson, Mark (1962–), 5–6
Lefebvre, Henri (1901–91), 10, 66

Lehmann, Hans-Thies, 62
liveness, 11, 48, 64
Lord of Misrule, 28–9

Marlowe, Christopher (1564–93), 56–57
mediaeval drama, 56
memory, 7, 44
    collective, 53
    motor, 47
    of past performances, 52
    sensory, 47
    see also emotional memory
Merleau-Ponty, Maurice (1908–61), 9
metronome, 16, 46, 59, 63
months, 54
Moon, 20, 54

Nashe, Thomas (1567–*c*.1601), 26–27
Natya Sastra, 19
Nemirovich-Danchenko, Vladimir (1858–1943), 1, 3
Newton, Isaac (1643–1727), 58
night-time, 26
now, 8, 15, 52

pauses, 33
Pepys, Samuel (1633–1703), 27
Phelan, Peggy (1948–), 48
phenomenology, 9
Plato (*c*.428–*c*.348 BCE), 15, 17
post-structuralism, 10
presence, 8, 61

pulse, 30
punctuation, 35
Pythagoras (c.570–c.495 BCE), 56, 61

real time, 57
Reiss, Anya (1991–), 5
rhythm
    arrhythmia, 16
    breath, 6
    circadian, 18
    collapsed into pitch or timbre, 63
    contagious effect, 17, 37
    dialogue, 7
    inner, 37
    modern life, 6
    movement, 15, 31
    polyrhythmia, 13, 20
    tempo-rhythm, 36, 45
rhythmanalysis, 10, 66
Roach, Joseph, 48
Roman theatre, 54
Rosa, Hartmut (1965–), 57–58

Schechner, Richard (1934–), 43–44
Schneider, Rebecca, 49
seasons, 21–22
sentence structures, 6
Shakespeare, William (1564–1616), 4, 53
    Hamlet, 32–33, 35
    Twelfth Night, 24–29
Smolin, Lee (1955–), 67

sound, speed of, 64
space and time, 60, 65–66
Stanislavski, Konstantin (1863–1938), 1, 4, 12–14, 35–37, 45–46, 59
    method, 51
Steele, Joshua (c.1700–96), 31–34
Stockhausen, Karlheinz (1928–2007), 61–66
Strasberg, Lee (1901–82), 46, 52
Sunday, 19, 26, 55

tactus, 34
Taylor, Diana, 48
tenses of acting, 51
time
    acceleration of, 57–59
    astrological, 56, 61
    Catholic and Protestant, 56
    contemporary sense of, 57, 60, 66
    cosmic, 18, 20, 57, 65
    cyclic, 2, 20, 23
    existence of, 2, 8
    historical, 1, 10
    polyrhythmic, 24
    real, 21
    sacred, 21
    spatial metaphors of, 2
    see also body and time; space and time
timing, 3, 32, 33, 37, 63

unity of time, 55

verse, 7, 32–35
Vick, Graham (1953–), 61, 65

walking, 31, 33, 40
week, 55, 61
Wooster Group, 7

yin and yang, 19
Young Vic, 13–14

Zeami Motokiyo (1363–1443),
    19
Zerubavel, Eviatar, 53